RUSSIA

Cath Senker

The
LAND
and the
PEOPLE

WAYLAND
www.waylandbooks.co.uk

First published in Great Britain in 2016 by Wayland

Editors: Nicola Edwards
Design: Dave Ball and Angela Ball at D&A
Cover design: D&A
Map artist: Stefan Chabluk

ISBN: 978 0 7502 9813 1
10 9 8 7 6 5 4 3 2 1

MIX
Paper from
responsible sources
FSC
www.fsc.org
FSC® C104740

Wayland, an imprint of
Hachette Children's Group
Part of Hodder and Stoughton
Carmelite House
50 Victoria Embankment
London EC4Y 0DZ

An Hachette UK Company
www.hachette.co.uk
www.hachettechildrens.co.uk

Printed in China

Picture acknowledgements: All images and graphic elements courtesy of Shutterstock except p6bl and p33bWikimedia Commons, p6br, p9br, p18t, p23br, p30bl, p34b, p36br, p36r, p41t and p43b Corbis

CONTENTS

RUSSIA ON THE MAP

Russia is vast. The largest country on Earth, it covers over one-ninth of the land and stretches across Europe and Asia. Russia has dense forests, high mountain peaks, sandy beaches and snowy winter landscapes.

Highs and lows

Over the last century, Russia has endured massive shocks: huge losses in both world wars, revolution, civil war, famine and the birth of the Soviet Union, the first communist country. It has experienced industrialisation at a furious pace, government terror and the complete collapse of the communist system. Yet Russia has been a world leader in culture, sport and space exploration. Since 1991, it has risen from the ashes of the Soviet Union to become one of the richest and most powerful countries in the world.

Russia fact file

Population: 142, 423, 773 (July 2015 est.)

Area: 17 million sq km

Capital city: Moscow

Highest peak: Mount Elbrus – 5,642m

Main language: Russian, written in Cyrillic alphabet

Currency: ruble

Whistlestop Russia

A few things to do on a trip to Russia...

⌃ Go to the Bolshoi Ballet in Moscow.

⌃ Travel in style on the Trans-Siberian railway.

⌃ Enjoy a snowy horse-drawn sleigh ride.

⌃ Relax at the Black Sea coast.

« Russia has borders with 14 countries and the longest coastline in the world, running along part of the Arctic and Pacific oceans and 14 seas.

R U S S I A

Sea of

Okhotsk

Pacific

Ocean

Sea of

Japan

CHINA

MONGOLIA

NORTH
KOREA

CHINA

A TUMULTUOUS HISTORY

From the 16th to the 20th century, Russia was an enormous empire ruled by tsars (emperors). At the peak of society was a tiny group of wealthy people, while the great majority eked out a miserable living on the land. In 1917, the tsar was overthrown in the Russian Revolution. In 1922, Russia formed a group of republics called the Union of Soviet Socialist Republics (USSR).

↑ Vladimir Lenin, a leader of the Russian Revolution

Stalin: 'man of steel'

The new communist government aimed to create a fairer society. But by 1929 Joseph Stalin had seized almost total power. He forced the USSR to build industries at an astonishing pace and seized farmers' land, making them join collective (shared) farms.

≫ Soviet tanks fighting the Germans in World War II

≪ Stalin. Anyone who opposed him came to a nasty end – he used his secret police force to murder his enemies.

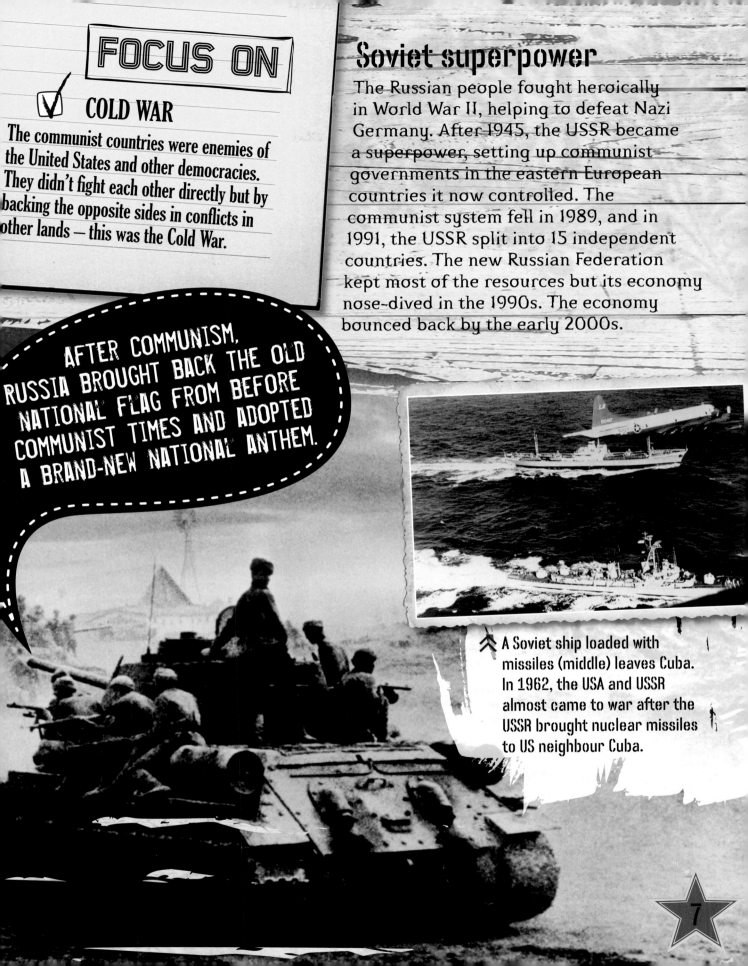

The communist countries were enemies of the United States and other democracies. They didn't fight each other directly but by backing the opposite sides in conflicts in other lands — this was the Cold War.

Soviet superpower

The Russian people fought heroically in World War II, helping to defeat Nazi Germany. After 1945, the USSR became a superpower, setting up communist governments in the eastern European countries it now controlled. The communist system fell in 1989, and in 1991, the USSR split into 15 independent countries. The new Russian Federation kept most of the resources but its economy nose-dived in the 1990s. The economy bounced back by the early 2000s.

AFTER COMMUNISM, RUSSIA BROUGHT BACK THE OLD NATIONAL FLAG FROM BEFORE COMMUNIST TIMES AND ADOPTED A BRAND-NEW NATIONAL ANTHEM.

⚔ A Soviet ship loaded with missiles (middle) leaves Cuba. In 1962, the USA and USSR almost came to war after the USSR brought nuclear missiles to US neighbour Cuba.

RUSSIA'S MELTING POT

Although four-fifths of the population are Russian, more than 120 ethnic groups live in Russia, most from neighbouring countries. It's partly because under Soviet rule, people moved around the USSR to work, often marrying locals and raising families. After 1991, some moved back to their birth country but others stayed in their adopted land.

Population fall

Russia's population fell dramatically in the 1990s, from 149 million in 1991 to 143 million in 2010. People were having fewer children, and Russian men have a particularly low life expectancy – many drink far too much alcohol, which damages their health.

>> Homelessness soared in the 1990s and remains a problem.

Famous Russians

Piotr Ilich Tchaikovsky (1840-93), composer

Leo Tolstoy (1828-1910) writer, author of War and Peace

Garry Kasparov, chess player

Anna Kournikova, tennis player, former model, trainer

8

RUSSIA HAS MORE IMMIGRANTS THAN ANY OTHER COUNTRY EXCEPT THE USA.

Immigrants

People have flocked to Russia to fill the gaps in the workforce, working on building sites, in markets and restaurants. While most are from the former USSR, others journey from China and the poorer lands of Central Asia, seeking a better life.

« Migrants from Central Asia often labour on building sites.

FOCUS ON

☑ PARENTAL GLORY

From 2009, the population started to rise again. The government has brought in healthy lifestyle programmes to persuade people to steer clear of alcohol. It encourages couples to have more children by offering better maternity pay. There are even awards for big families: parents with seven or more children receive an Order of Parental Glory!

« President Putin (centre) presents the Order of Parental Glory to a family with seven children, in 2015.

A LAND OF CONTRASTS

^ The Ural Mountains run south to the Ural River.

As well as an incredible variety of scenery, Russia has every climate zone except tropical. In the summer, people lounge on the sunny beaches of the Black Sea. In contrast, the 'Wild East' of Siberia is the coldest inhabited place in the world. Winter temperatures drop to a staggering -60° C.

« Lake Baikal freezes from January to May or June.

Landscapes

Lake Baikal is the world's oldest and deepest freshwater lake: it's 1,642m to the bottom – that's over 1km deep! The longest river is the River Lena. The Ural Mountains straddle Russia from North to South for 2,500 km, forming the boundary between Europe and Asia. All the known chemical elements on Earth are found there.

^ In the summer, people flock to the sunny beaches of the Black Sea.

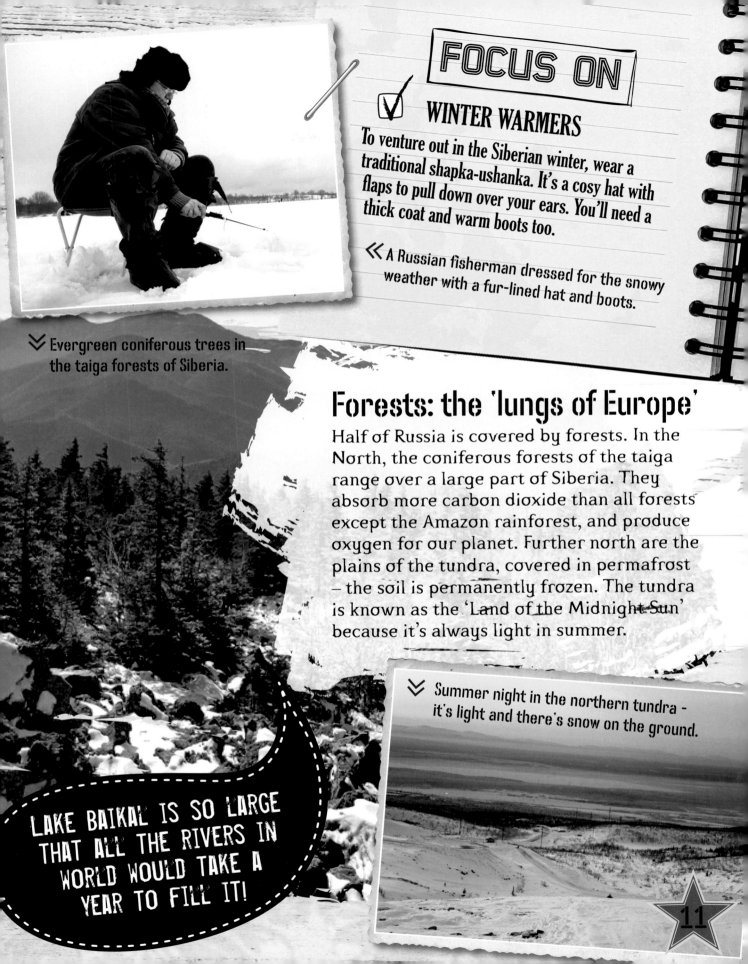

✓ WINTER WARMERS

To venture out in the Siberian winter, wear a traditional shapka-ushanka. It's a cosy hat with flaps to pull down over your ears. You'll need a thick coat and warm boots too.

≪ A Russian fisherman dressed for the snowy weather with a fur-lined hat and boots.

⌄ Evergreen coniferous trees in the taiga forests of Siberia.

Forests: the 'lungs of Europe'

Half of Russia is covered by forests. In the North, the coniferous forests of the taiga range over a large part of Siberia. They absorb more carbon dioxide than all forests except the Amazon rainforest, and produce oxygen for our planet. Further north are the plains of the tundra, covered in permafrost – the soil is permanently frozen. The tundra is known as the 'Land of the Midnight Sun' because it's always light in summer.

⌄ Summer night in the northern tundra - it's light and there's snow on the ground.

LAKE BAIKAL IS SO LARGE THAT ALL THE RIVERS IN WORLD WOULD TAKE A YEAR TO FILL IT!

GO WILD IN RUSSIA

Russia's wildlife is adapted to survive in its extreme habitats. In the chilly tundra, mosses, lichens and grasses hug close to the ground. Arctic foxes have short, rounded ears to reduce heat loss and fur-covered soles to keep their feet cosy. A long, thick, shaggy coat of long brown hair protects musk oxen (right). Reindeer simply avoid the tundra winter by heading for the forests.

⌃ Arctic foxes turn white in winter for camouflage against the snow.

Taiga forest

The taiga woodlands are home to small mammals, including sable and ermine (weasels), and squirrels. Foxes, bears and wolves hunt elk and deer. Foxes and wolves also roam the steppes. There's little natural shelter, but marmots, mice and other burrowing animals can make a quick get-away from predators underground.

« Moose live in the floodplains (flat areas) of the taiga.

Lake Baikal

Lake Baikal is a unique habitat. It's home to the earless nerpa, the only seal that lives in fresh water. It can stay underwater for up to an hour and dive down to 300m. It's a mystery how seals reached Lake Baikal, hundreds of kilometres from the sea. Another unusual resident is the golomyanka fish; instead of laying eggs, it gives birth to live young.

« The extraordinary earless nerpa seal of Lake Baikal.

The grasslands, the vast grassy areas of southern Russia, are called the steppe.

AROUND TWO-THIRDS OF THE 1,700 SPECIES OF PLANTS AND ANIMALS IN LAKE BAIKAL ARE FOUND NOWHERE ELSE ON EARTH.

FOCUS ON

☑ **SAVE THE SIBERIAN TIGER**

The WWF Tiger Youth Forum is an international group of youth ambassadors who raise awareness among young people of the need to save the tigers. They protest against illegal hunting. In Russia, the Siberian tiger was dying out, but campaigners are pushing for the Tx2 goal to double numbers of wild tigers from 2010 to 2022.

» The number of Siberian tigers in Russia is rising again.

RICH RESOURCES

Russia is one of the world's fastest-growing economies. It is blessed with vast resources of oil, gas and minerals: coal, metals, diamonds and gold. Russia sells more gas than any other country and is the second largest oil exporter after Saudi Arabia. Russia has influence over other countries because they rely on its oil and gas supplies.

⌃ A car assembly plant in Tatarsta
Russia. Luxury Western vehicles
popular with wealthy Russians.

'Resource curse'

Yet Russia suffers from the 'resource curse'. Its economy yoyos up and down with oil prices. In 2008, the world price of oil plummeted, and Russia was plunged into crisis. In 2011, oil prices rose again and the economy recovered. The government paid back some money it owed and unemployment fell. But prices swooped down again in 2015.

⌄ An oil tanker carries
fuel from the oil
fields of Siberia.

⌄ Oil pumps in Russia

Industry and services

Heavy industry is big business, especially metals, machine building, transport equipment and chemicals. Service industries are growing too – including tourism. Visitors cruise in steamships on the Volga River, enjoy bird watching around Lake Baikal or visit the country's world-class galleries and museums.

⌃ The Hermitage Museum in St Petersburg is Russia's largest art gallery.

OIL, GAS AND MINERALS MAKE UP FOUR-FIFTHS OF RUSSIA'S EXPORTS.

FOCUS ON

☑ EMISSIONS AND THE ENVIRONMENT

With all that heavy industry, Russia is the biggest producer of carbon dioxide emissions after China and the USA. In 2015, it promised to reduce emissions by 25-30 per cent below the 1990 level by 2030. However, climate experts say it must do more to clean up its act.

« Critics say Russian factory owners are not doing enough to prevent air pollution.

ON THE MOVE

Russia's major cities are gridlocked with traffic, but many areas of the country lack paved roads. Just a third of Russians have a car. People usually travel by train, and most goods trundle through the country on freight trains.

⌃ A typical traffic jam in Moscow.

Trans-Siberian Railway

The longest railway in the world, the Trans-Siberian Railway stretches 9,288km from Moscow in the West to Vladivostok in the East. It transports oil, coal, metals, diamonds and gold to western Russia. Passengers spend the six-day journey in a comfortable train compartment. At night they are lulled to sleep by the gentle rocking of the train.

≫ The Trans-Siberian Railway also has a route to China.

Underground palaces

To get around Moscow and St Petersburg, go underground. Moscow's speedy metro system carries an astounding 9.5 million passengers daily. The stations are richly decorated like palaces or museums. Their walls and columns are often made from coloured marble and covered with paintings, mosaics and sculptures.

« Chandeliers glitter above the platforms at the beautiful Komsomolskaya Metro station in Moscow.

FOCUS ON

☑ **SPACE RACE**

Russia has been a leader in space technology since Soviet times. Yuri Gagarin was the first man to orbit Earth in 1961, and two years later, Valentina Tereshkova was the first woman in space. Nowadays, the Russian Space Agency promotes space tourism. If you have £13–26 million to spend, you could travel by spacecraft to the International Space Station, 400km above Earth.

« The Russian 'Progress' spacecraft prepares for lift-off on a mission to carry cargo to the International Space Station in 2010.

17

ON THE LAND

Life on the land in most countries tends to change at a snail's pace – but not in Russia. Under Soviet rule, the collective farms had to hand over all their produce to the government. Farmers couldn't see the point of working hard only to give away all their crops, so the farms did badly. Now, many collective farms are run as companies or cooperatives.

⌃ A welcome lunch break at a collective farm in the Kiev region, in 1936

From land and sea

Most farmland is used for raising crops. Wheat, barley, rye and oats fill the grasslands, while millet and melons grow along the lower River Volga. Beef cattle and pigs are kept for their meat. Russia has long coastlines, and fishing is a good source of income. With the largest forest reserves in world, Russian loggers are busy exporting timber, paper and other wood products.

⌃ A huge timber carrier transports logs. Russia has around one-quarter of all the world's trees.

⌄ A fishing boat in Sochi, on the Black Sea coast

WITH MUCH OF RUSSIA'S TERRITORY A FROZEN WASTELAND, JUST 13 PER CENT OF THE LAND IS USED FOR AGRICULTURE.

All change

After a decade of decline in the 1990s, farming grew impressively. Since 2000, huge farms have developed, the biggest owned by foreign companies. There's a government scheme to modernize agriculture by 2020. It aims to attract more foreign businesses and to cultivate unused land.

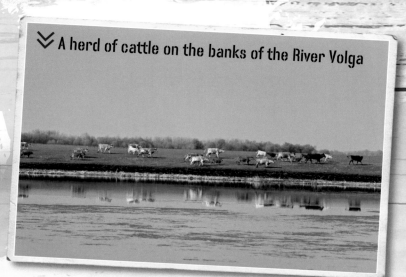
≫ A herd of cattle on the banks of the River Volga

FOCUS ON

✓ GROW YOUR OWN

People in Russia have always enjoyed growing their own fruit and vegetables on a small plot. These plots often kept them alive under communism and are still popular today. Nearly two-thirds of people living in cities have a vegetable garden or an allotment at their dacha.

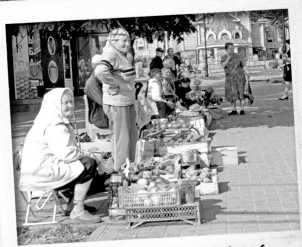
≫ Elderly women often sell produce from their allotments by the roadside.

19

MODERNISING MOSCOW

About three-quarters of Russians live in cities. The capital, Moscow, is Russia's largest city by far. With its brightly painted onion-shaped domes, St Basil's Cathedral is easily the most famous building. The Kremlin has ornate cathedrals and grand palaces and is home to the president.

⟰ St Basil's Cathedral is now a museum for tourists.

Building and business

In recent years, Moscow has been one big construction site. Old Soviet-era hotels have been knocked to the ground while the Cathedral of Christ the Saviour has been rebuilt. The Moscow International Business Centre, still under development, includes the Mercury City tower, the tallest tower in Europe at 339m. The Manezh shopping centre has shot up next to Red Square, full of shops and restaurants.

≫ Shoppers at a traditional weekend vegetable market in Moscow.

Crowded communalki

Many new homes have also been built, but the surge in population means there's a shortage of housing. Most people occupy tiny flats in tall apartment blocks. Large numbers still live in communalki – Soviet-style apartments, where families have one bedroom each and share the kitchen and bathroom. Nowadays, most people want a private flat even though it costs more.

⋙ The Krasnogorsk housing development – brand-new high-rise blocks packed closely together.

⋙ Moscow International Business Centre, with the Mercury City tower on the far left

MOSCOW'S POPULATION IS 11.5 MILLION AND RISING.

FOCUS ON

✓ **RED SQUARE**

Under Soviet rule, Moscow's Red Square was filled with thousands of soldiers parading in neat rows to celebrate Workers' Day on 1 May. In 2008, the celebration was restored, but for Victory Day on 9 May, to mark the end of World War II.

⋀ Victory Day fireworks light up Red Square.

ST PETERSBURG

Russia's second city, St Petersburg, was the country's capital for two centuries until the Russian Revolution (see pages 6-7). Less than half the size of Moscow, it's a significant historical and cultural centre and a major port. St Petersburg is known as 'Venice of the North', after the Italian city built on a network of canals. It too has many canals, and no fewer than 342 bridges.

≫ A ballet performance at the Mariinsky Theatre in St Petersburg.

City of culture

Peter the Great's successors brought European architects to design elegant palaces and cathedrals, so the city is full of beautiful historic buildings. The magnificent Hermitage Museum houses some of the world's greatest art collections. St Petersburg also has the best of Russian contemporary art and it's the place for top-class ballet and opera.

≪ The extraordinary Hermitage Museum, which houses a mind-boggling 3 million items!

Dvors

St Petersburg is an intriguing mix of old and new. Huge modern shopping centres have been constructed in recent years. But step through arched entrances on the main streets and you can find yourself in a dvor – an old-fashioned enclosed courtyard, with buildings unchanged for decades.

« A view of the sky from an enclosed courtyard – some dvors lead on one to another.

⌄ A view of St Isaac's Cathedral in St Petersburg. The canals in the city centre are lined with Italian-style mansions to add to the likeness with Venice.

FOCUS ON

WHITE NIGHTS

During the long summer evenings, it barely gets dark at night. On these White Nights, festivals are held in the concert halls, and everyone parties until late.

⌃ People enjoy salsa dancing as part of a White Nights festival in St Petersburg.

LOOKING AT EVERY EXHIBIT IN THE HERMITAGE FOR A MINUTE WOULD TAKE 11 YEARS!

RAISED IN RUSSIA

Russian children can think themselves lucky they didn't grow up in Soviet times. Rote learning was common – teachers expected pupils to memorise lots of facts. Nowadays, they encourage creative thinking so children can solve problems.

Study and training

Children start school aged seven. At 16, they decide whether to carry on with academic subjects and study for another two or three years for their secondary-level certificate. If they're eager to learn a trade instead, they can switch to vocational (work-based) training.

⩔ Even young primary school children sit formally at desks in rows.

⩓ As well as the basic subjects, children can do art at school.

⩓ Schools are investing in computers – these children are making a robot.

MOST RUSSIAN CHILDREN WEAR A SMART SCHOOL UNIFORM.

FOCUS ON

✓ **FAVOURITE ACTIVITIES**

Gymnastics and ballet are top choices. Children start ballet at five and often dance alongside adults in performances. Many young people sing in a 'хор' (say 'hop') or choir, sometimes performing in traditional costume. They sing everything from classical pieces to folk and pop. Chess is taken seriously in Russia; lots of children join clubs and compete in tournaments.

⌃ Playing chess on the streets at a sports society celebration in Moscow.

⌃ Joining a sports club is popular. These boys are competing at a stadium event.

The school day

The school day is from 8 a.m. until 1 or 2 p.m. Main subjects include Russian literature and language, maths, history, geography, the sciences and PE. Children from ethnic minorities study in their own language but learn Russian at secondary school. After school, there's a choice of extra activities, including dancing, sports, singing, painting and crafts. Many children attend Youth Club after school, at the weekend and in school holidays to make friends and learn new skills.

CHILLING OUT

Winter weather doesn't stop Russians from having fun. They take to the ice and go skating, skiing and sledging. Ice hockey is popular too. Players wear a helmet because this fast-moving sport can be dangerous – no one wants to fall and crack their head on the ice.

» You can go skiing or snowboarding at one of Russia's many ski resorts.

ICE HOCKEY IS ONE OF RUSSIA'S FAVOURITE SPORTS AND THE NATIONAL TEAM IS HIGHLY SUCCESSFUL.

» The competition is fierce in this ice hockey tournament.

Summer pastimes

When the warm weather finally comes, people head outdoors to enjoy tennis, jogging or swimming. They walk in the countryside or fish in the lakes. Elderly people play chess and dominoes in the park.

« Children in giant transparent balls enjoy zorbing on a lake in Novgorod.

» Russians love to spend time tending their vegetable patches.

Days at the dacha

Although more Russians holiday abroad than they used to, the majority have a 'staycation'. Most families in cities have access to a dacha – a wooden summer house by a lake, river or the sea. They spend their summer holidays there, growing fruit and vegetables, enjoying the fresh air and having barbecues. Often, there's no running water so they fetch it from a well or village pump.

FOCUS ON

☑ **STORY TELLING**

The long, dark evenings create the perfect atmosphere for story telling. A favourite character in children's fairy tales is witch Baba Yaga, who lives in a house raised on chicken legs and flies around in a mortar (heavy bowl), scaring people. Many fairy tales were collected and written down by the poet Alexsandr Pushkin (1799–1837).

« A sculpture of Baba Yaga; in stories she is wise and powerful as well as scary.

27

RELIGIOUS REVIVAL

Under communism, religion was banned and it was impossible to follow Christian customs openly. Since Russia's independence, there's been a huge surge in religious fervour among all ages. Old churches have been repaired and many new ones built. Like churches, mosques have mushroomed since 1991, when there were only 300. By 2015 there were more than 8,000. Islam is Russia's second most popular religion.

A spiritual experience

On Sunday, bells from the splendid blue or gold-domed Orthodox church call the people to prayer. In the decorative interior, the atmosphere is warm and inviting. Hundreds of people pack into the church and go to kiss icons and light candles in front of them. It's all part of the spiritual experience of the Orthodox Church. After the service, people take home bottles of holy water, which they believe cures all manner of illnesses.

≫ Opened in 2015, Moscow Cathedral Mosque is the city's main mosque.

≪ Trinity Lavra, near Moscow, the most important monastery (monks' home) of the Russian Orthodox Church – with typical blue and gold domes.

ABOUT 10-15 PER CENT OF THE RUSSIAN POPULATION ARE MUSLIMS.

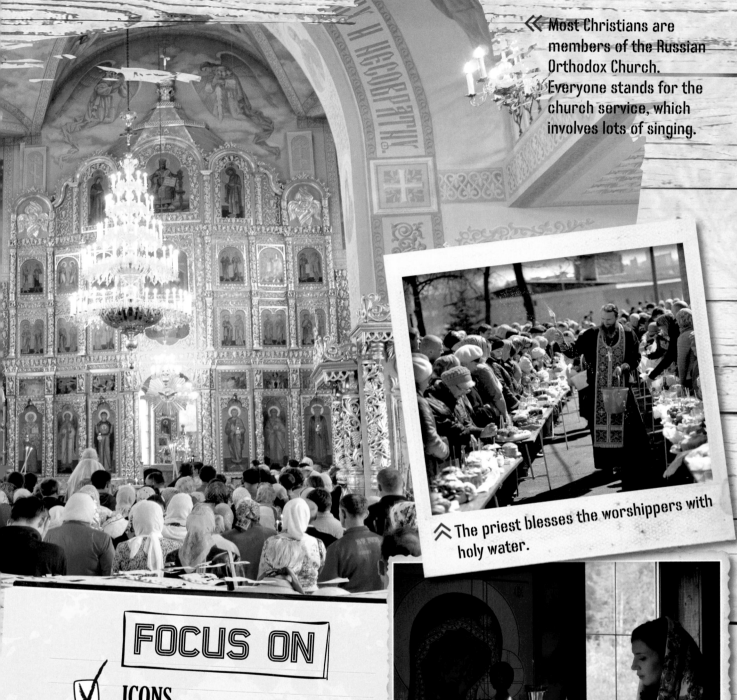

« Most Christians are members of the Russian Orthodox Church. Everyone stands for the church service, which involves lots of singing.

⌃ The priest blesses the worshippers with holy water.

FOCUS ON

☑ ICONS

Russian Orthodox churches have a solid screen decorated with icons — religious paintings, usually on wood, showing scenes from the Bible or the lives of saints. These holy objects are a vital element in worship. On festival days, the priest and worshippers carry icons in a procession around the church.

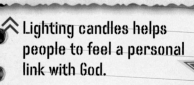

⌃ Lighting candles helps people to feel a personal link with God.

FESTIVAL FUN

New Year is Russia's biggest festival. On New Year's Eve, families gather for a special dinner. At 11.55 p.m., the president addresses the nation. The Kremlin clock chimes at midnight (main picture), the national anthem plays, and in cities, fireworks light up the night sky.

⌃ Musicians on a street stage during the Pancake Week celebrations.

Christmas

Religious festivals have made a huge comeback. Orthodox Christmas is celebrated on 7 January. The night before, people eat a delicious rich meal of 12 dishes, called Holy Supper.

⌃ People gather in Moscow to celebrate Christmas Eve.

RUSSIAN CHILDREN RECEIVE NEW YEAR'S GIFTS FROM GRANDFATHER FROST AND THE SNOW MAIDEN, THE RUSSIAN VERSION OF FATHER CHRISTMAS.

Pancake feasts

Maslenitsa (Pancake Week) is a week of feasting before Lent. It's a time for snowball fights, sleigh rides, celebrations and dancing in traditional costumes and, of course, eating pancakes. These tasty treats are eaten to celebrate the start of spring. The shape of the pancake stands for the sun. Russians enjoy their pancakes with sour cream, melted butter, jam or caviar (fish eggs).

>> Pancakes served with caviar, sour cream and jam – delicious!

FOCUS ON

✓ **EASTER EGGS**

Easter eggs aren't always made from chocolate! In Russia, people exchange beautifully decorated eggs at Easter. Some are real ones, dipped in colourful dye. Others are made from wood, painted with flowers, churches or bright patterns.

>> One of the famous Easter eggs made by jeweller Peter Carl Fabergé (1846–1920) for the royal family.

31

COUNTRY OF CULTURE

Russia is famous for its top-notch literature, theatre, classical music, ballet and art. Perhaps you've heard of Leo Tolstoy's 'Anna Karenina' (1875-7) or his epic 'War and Peace' (1865-9), made into a BBC TV drama in 2015. Fyodor Dostoevsky wrote the gripping detective story 'Crime and Punishment' (1866).

⌃ A portrait of the author Leo Tolstoy, in 1873.

19th-century classics

Check the performances at a major theatre or concert hall, and it's likely a great 19th-century Russian work will appear. Anton Chekhov is famous for his realistic plays, including 'The Seagull' (1896) and 'The Cherry Orchard' (1904). His strong characters struggled to cope with the changes in their lives and society. People can still relate to those issues today. Piotr Ilich Tchaikovsky (1840–93) is probably Russia's best-known composer.

« An abstract painting by one of Russia's best-known artists, Vasily Kandinsky (1866-1944), on a French stamp.

⌃ Keira Knightley starred in a film of Anna Karenina in 2012.

FOCUS ON

✓ BEAUTIFUL BALLET

Ballet was introduced to Russia in the 17th century to entertain the tsar. Russian enthusiasm for this dance form grew, and by the 20th century, Russian ballet companies were touring the world. Today, you have to grab tickets for the hugely successful Bolshoi and Mariinsky Ballet months in advance.

⌃ Tchaikovsky wrote the music for ballets including Swan Lake (above), Sleeping Beauty and The Nutcracker.

MUSIC FROM TCHAIKOVSKY'S NUTCRACKER SUITE FEATURED IN THE 1940 DISNEY ANIMATED FILM FANTASIA.

Communist control

Under Soviet rule, artists and playwrights could not express themselves freely. They were expected to show the glorious march of communism, with strong workers happily tilling the land and labouring in the factories. The grip of Soviet control on the arts loosened in the 1980s.

⌄ An old statue of labourers dating back to the Soviet era.

⌃ Aleksandr Solzhenitsyn (1908–2008) was forced into exile for writing books that criticised the government.

33

NEW RUSSIA, NEW CULTURE

Since the fall of the Soviet Union, a world of new Russian culture has opened up. To promote the country's new image, the government encourages Russian writers. The top literature competition is the Russian Booker Prize with a generous prize for the winner. The Read Russia scheme publishes Russian authors in other languages.

⌃ Traditional matryoshka – Russian dolls – including ones of President Putin.

New writers

From the 1990s, writers such as Aleksandra Marinina and Viktor Dotsenko set their stories in the shadowy underworld of Russia's gangs. Marinina's novels have a strong female detective lead, Anastasia Kamenskaya. Fantasy and sci fi have taken off too. Dmitrii Glukhovskii's 'Metro2033' depicts a future dystopia (horrible world) where everyone lives in the Metro because nuclear war has destroyed the world above.

'METRO2033' WAS TURNED INTO AN XBOX VIDEO GAME.

⌄ Marinina's novels were turned into a popular TV series.

New music

New Russian music has exploded on to the scene. Singer-songwriter Nyusha and the rock band Slot are big stars, yet they're barely known outside Russia. Even there, most young people listen to Western music. In contrast, some of the world's best classical musicians come from Russia.

△ Girl band Propaganda perform on stage in a Moscow club.

⌄ Opened in 2015, Garace Contemporary Culture Centre is in Gorky Park, Moscow.

FOCUS ON

☑ **GOING TO THE MOVIES**

Government funding for film-making disappeared along with the Soviet Union. Since 2005, the Russian film industry has revived, with some government support. Multi-screen complexes have sprouted up in major cities, and cinema audiences are growing. But it's foreign films most people come to see, especially the latest Hollywood blockbusters.

△ Moscow International Film Festival is held every year and awards prizes to some of the world's top film makers.

SPORT MAD

In the days of communism, the Soviet government promoted sport to show the superiority of its political system. Although communism is long gone, Russians are as enthusiastic about sport as ever.

Medal winners

Russia has enjoyed incredible success in gymnastics, tennis and athletics. Talented young gymnasts go to Moscow Children's Palace of Culture and Sport for training. Maria Sharapova was the first Russian to win Wimbledon in 2004, aged just 17. Since 1996, Russia has won more medals at the Olympic Games than all other countries except the USA. But in 2015, Russia was banned from international athletics competitions, accused of allowing athletes to use drugs to improve their performance.

AFTER THE 2012 OLYMPICS, ALL 129 RUSSIAN MEDALLISTS WERE GIVEN A BRAND-NEW AUDI CAR.

≪ Maria Sharapova

⌃ A talented young gymnast in training at the Dynamo club in Moscow.

<< Fans of Spartak Moscow, one of Russia's most successful football teams.

Football fanatics

Football is the top spectator sport in Russia. Favourite clubs include Zenit from St Petersburg and its rival Dynamo from Moscow. Kids dream of playing for one of these teams. Wealthy Russians have pumped money into major clubs to buy foreign players and managers to up their game, and have purchased foreign clubs. In 2003, Roman Abramovich bought English club Chelsea. Russia was to host the FIFA World Cup in 2018.

FOCUS ON

☑ **SOCHI 2014**

In 2014, Russia hosted the Winter Olympics in the southern city of Sochi. The competition was held against a background of poor management, corruption, security threats and political unrest in nearby Ukraine. In the end, the event passed off peacefully, and Russia won the most medals.

⌄ The Olympic Park in Sochi, just before the opening ceremony of the 2014 Olympics.

⌃ Russia's Mariya Savinova expresses her joy as she wins the gold medal in the women's 800 metres final at the London 2012 Olympics.

BLINIS AND BORSCHT

Living in a chilly climate, Russians love warming foods with plenty of carbs. They tuck into hot, filling dishes, usually home cooked with locally grown beetroot, cabbage and potatoes. Russians eat potatoes most days, and there's always dark, chewy rye bread on the table.

Pickled vegetables, including chillies, peppers and cucumbers, on sale at a farmers' market.

Hearty food

For a traditional Russian breakfast, people eat kasha (porridge), a sandwich, eggs or cereal. Lunch is the main meal. Many cafes and restaurants offer a cheap lunchtime menu: soup; meat with potatoes or porridge; and tea or coffee. Families gather for dinner around 7 p.m., often in front of the TV. Dinner is usually a meat dish, perhaps with Russian salad, made from potatoes, mayonnaise and vegetables. It's followed by a cup of sweet tea.

RUSSIANS ADORE PICKLED ZAKUSKI (APPETIZERS) SUCH AS PICKLED CUCUMBERS, MUSHROOMS AND HERRING.

A bowl of tasty borscht.

Russian salad

Top treats

Other popular dishes include borscht, a deep red beetroot soup eaten hot or cold with sour cream, dill and rye bread. Blinis are thin pancakes with butter, sour cream, jam or caviar added for flavour.

A batch of blinis served with caviar and sour cream.

Pelmeni (dumplings) can be stuffed with meat, fish or mushrooms.

FOCUS ON

✓ THE SAMOVAR

In the old days, Russians lit charcoal under this metal urn to heat water for drinking tea whenever they fancied. A stand on top kept the teapot hot. Nowadays, many people use electric samovars or kettles.

A modern electric samovar

RULING RUSSIA

R ussia's government has undergone extraordinary changes. After the Soviet state crumbled, there were the beginnings of democracy – lots of new political parties popped up. Yet within just a few years, a powerful leader ruled Russia once again.

President Putin

Since 2000, Vladimir Putin, the leader of the United Russia party, has been president, except for in 2008–12 when Prime Minister Dmitry Medvedev took over the job. Many Russians fiercely support their president and believe he's making Russia strong and proud again. Others who oppose the government struggle to make their voices heard. Since 2012, Putin has introduced many laws to limit protest, including fines and prison sentences.

≫ A demonstration in Ukraine in 2014 against Russia sending troops to Crimea.

IN 2012, MEDVEDEV AND PUTIN SIMPLY SWAPPED ROLES: PUTIN BECAME PRESIDENT AGAIN AND MEDVEDEV PRIME MINISTER.

⌃ Punk band Pussy Riot, sentenced to prison for illegally performing a song in Moscow's Cathedral of Christ the Saviour, 2012.

⌃ A 2008 election poster with Putin and Medvedev: 'Together We Will Win'.

FOCUS ON

☑ **FIGHTING WITH THE NEIGHBOURS**

Since the fall of the Soviet Union, Russia has tried to keep the republics of the Russian Federation together. But Chechnya wanted independence and rebelled against Russia from 1991. Violent conflict between the rebels and government continued until 2009. In 2014, Putin seized Crimea, a part of Ukraine with mostly Russian inhabitants, saying he needed to protect Russian interests. His actions angered the USA and European Union, who introduced sanctions to limit trade with Russia.

⌄ Russian soldiers rest between battles with Chechen rebels, 2000.

THE 'RUSSIAN IDEA'

Russians are proud of their nation and values and have a strong sense of identity. They believe in their spiritual existence, sense of community and links with the land. For example, they keep up the age-old tradition of picking mushrooms and berries in the countryside. Most Russians feel they should keep up their traditions but also borrow from the 'best of the West'.

☆ Grandparents help to look after their grandchildren in the school holidays.

Winter sports

The cold climate is part of Russian identity. When the lakes freeze over, people go ice fishing and skating. They love skiing. For the truly brave, there's ice swimming. Known as morzhi (walruses), ice swimmers cut holes in the ice so they can immerse themselves in freezing-cold water. Brrrh!

☆ People travel specially from the cities to pick mushrooms.

RUSSIA HAS MORE THAN 200 KINDS OF EDIBLE MUSHROOMS BUT WATCH OUT FOR THE POISONOUS ONES!

Hot baths

To warm up, you can visit a Russian banya (sauna), another essential Russian experience. It's thought that the hot, damp steam helps to expel fat from the body and clean the skin.

> The birch brooms in the banya are for smacking cold water on to your body.

> An ice swimmer bravely bathing in a hole in the ice.

FOCUS ON

☑ ## THE DOWNSIDE

Some take pride in their nation to extremes and exclude others, calling for 'Russia for the Russians'. Far-right groups have carried out attacks on immigrants, unfairly blaming them for the increase in crime in cities. And some believe that Russian values don't include accepting lesbian and gay people. In 2013 a law was passed against homosexuality. This has fuelled a rise in attacks on lesbians and gays.

⌃ People protest in support of lesbian and gay rights in St Petersburg, 2015.

LOOKING TO THE FUTURE

The heat's definitely on for Russia; climate change is a major challenge. Higher temperatures could melt the Siberian permafrost – handy for growing more food. But wilder weather could bring disastrous droughts and floods.

⌃ A heatwave in 2010 brought devastating forest and peat fires.

Renewable energy

The government is beginning to address climate change. In 2015, it introduced new measures to encourage the growth of renewable energy such as wind and solar power. Electricity companies were told to buy from renewable sources.

≫ Tourists visiting Intercession Cathedral in Red Square, Moscow in 2010. The city is covered in dense smoke from the burning forests.

≪ A mini solar power plant in a Moscow park. In 2015, many new solar projects were approved.

⚠ Nearly everyone in Russia has at least one mobile phone.

☑ **RUSSIA'S FRIENDS**

Russia is part of Europe and Asia. It doesn't want to be tied to any particular country politically but hopes to steer its own course, choosing which countries to ally with when it's useful. Sometimes, Russia is friendly with Europe and the USA, sometimes less so. One thing is certain: tensions are likely to continue while Russia has conflicts with its neighbours such as Ukraine.

Normal life

Despite upheavals and rapid change in Russia, most people live a 'normal' Western-style life. Two-thirds have jobs in service industries and a quarter work in industry. Around half the population use the Internet every day, and they love social media. Russians in the 21st century are likely to have a similar lifestyle to people in other developed countries.

⌄ Young people watch a show about electricity and magnetism at a science festival in St Petersburg.

SEVENTY PER CENT OF 17-22-YEAR-OLDS GO TO UNIVERSITY IN RUSSIA, COMPARED TO ABOUT 40 PER CENT IN THE USA.

QUIZ

How much do you know about Russia's land and people? Try this quick quiz and find out!

1 Which climate zone is not found in Russia?
a) Tundra
b) Tropical
c) Taiga

2 What are blinis?
a) Pickled cucumbers
b) Appetisers
c) Thin pancakes

3 What's unique about Lake Baikal?
a) Many of the species there are found nowhere else on Earth.
b) It's a long way from the sea.
c) It has fresh water.

4 What do most Russians do in the summer holidays?
a) Go on holiday abroad
b) Stay at home
c) Go to a dacha in the countryside

5 Where is St Basil's Cathedral?
a) St Petersburg
b) Moscow
c) Siberia

6 Which is the coldest place to live?
a) Siberia
b) St Petersburg
c) The Black Sea

7 When do Russians celebrate Orthodox Christmas?
a) 7 January
b) 24 December
c) 25 December

8 Who was Anton Chekhov?
a) A famous composer
b) A 19th-century artist
c) A popular playwright

True or false?
a) You can go by train from Russia to China.
b) The Ural Mountains are the highest in the world.
c) Nearly everyone in Russia has a car.

Answers: 1b, 2c, 3a, 4c, 5b, 6a, 7a, 8c;
True or false? aT, bF, cF

GLOSSARY

ambassador
A person who speaks on behalf of an international organisation or their country

civil war
War between groups in the same country

communist
A system in which the government owns and controls the means of production, such as farms and mines.

contemporary
Belonging to the present time

cooperative
A business owned and run by the people involved, with the profits shared by them

corruption
When people in charge behave dishonestly.

democracy
A political system in which all adults can vote in free elections for the rulers of the country.

emissions
Light, heat or gases that are sent out into the atmosphere.

empire
A group of countries that are controlled by one country.

ethnic group
A group of people who share culture, tradition, way of life and sometimes language.

freight
Goods that are transported by ships, planes, lorries or trains.

immigrant
A person who moves to settle in another country.

life expectancy
The number of years that a person is likely to live.

permafrost
A layer of soil that is permanently frozen, in very cold regions of the world.

renewable energy
Energy that is replaced naturally, such as energy from the wind and sun.

republic
Country ruled by a president

revolution
When a group of people organise to change the government of a country.

sanctions
An official order that limits trade and contacts with a particular country, in order to make it do something, such as obeying international law.

superpower
A country that has very great military or economic power and a lot of influence.

taiga
Forest that grows in wet ground in far northern regions of the earth.

time zone
One of the 24 areas that the world is divided into, each with its own time.

tundra
The large, flat Arctic regions of northern Europe, Asia and North America

Further information
Books

Countries Around the World: Russia by Jilly Hunt (Heinemann, 2012)

Developing World: Russia and Moscow by Philip Steele (Franklin Watts, 2016)

It's Cool to Learn About Countries: Russia by Katie Marsico (Kindle Edition; Cherry Lake Publishing, 2013)

R is for Russia by Vladimir Kabakov (Frances Lincoln Children's Books, 2013)

Russia: A Benjamin Blog and His Inquisitive Dog Guide by Anita Ganeri (Raintree, 2015)

Websites
Activity village: Russia
www.activityvillage.co.uk/russia

TIME for kids Russia
www.timeforkids.com/destination/russia

www.oxfam.org.uk/education/resources/your-world-my-world
Explores the lives of four children around the world, including Russia

Index